8/18

HOWARD and the MUMMY

Howard Carter and the Search for King Tut's Tomb

Tracey Fern
Pictures by Boris Kulikov

Farrar Straus Giroux
New York

To Sammy and Ali with love from their Mummy
—T.F.

For Max and André
—B.K.

Farrar Straus Giroux Books for Young Readers
An imprint of Macmillan Publishing Group, LLC
175 Fifth Avenue, New York, NY 10010

Text copyright © 2018 by Tracey Fern
Pictures copyright © 2018 by Boris Kulikov
All rights reserved
Printed in China by RR Donnelley Asia Printing Solutions Ltd.,
Dongguan City, Guangdong Province
Designed by Roberta Pressel
First edition, 2018
1 3 5 7 9 10 8 6 4 2

mackids.com

Library of Congress Cataloging-in-Publication Data

Names: Fern, Tracey E., author. | Kulikov, Boris, 1966– illustrator.
Title: Howard and the mummy : Howard Carter and the search for King Tut's
    tomb / Tracey Fern ; pictures by Boris Kulikov.
Description: First edition. | New York : Farrar Straus Giroux, 2018.
Identifiers: LCCN 2017011995 | ISBN 9780374303051 (hardcover)
Subjects: LCSH: Carter, Howard, 1874–1939—Juvenile literature. |
    Tutankhamen, King of Egypt—Tomb—Juvenile literature. |
    Egyptologists—Great Britain—Biography—Juvenile literature. |
    Excavations (Archaeology)—Egypt—Valley of the Kings—Juvenile
    literature. | Egypt—Antiquities—Juvenile literature.
Classification: LCC DT87.5 .F47 2018 | DDC 932.014—dc23
LC record available at https://lccn.loc.gov/2017011995

Our books may be purchased in bulk for promotional, educational, or business use.
Please contact your local bookseller or the Macmillan Corporate and Premium Sales Department
at (800) 221-7945 ext. 5442 or by e-mail at MacmillanSpecialMarkets@macmillan.com.

Howard Carter adored mummies. He got to know one quite well when he was a boy in England. Howard often visited a nearby mansion that was stuffed with a collection of ancient Egyptian artifacts: carved coffins, mysterious scrolls, magical statues, and—best of all—a marvelously shriveled, semi-decayed mummy.

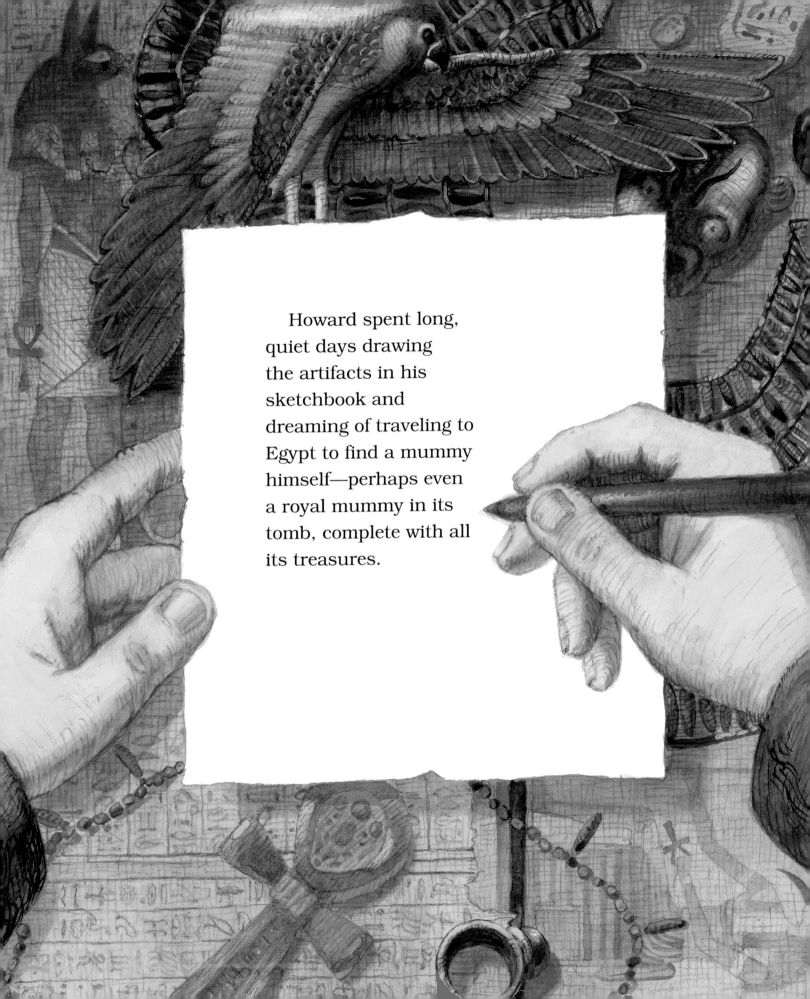

Howard spent long, quiet days drawing the artifacts in his sketchbook and dreaming of traveling to Egypt to find a mummy himself—perhaps even a royal mummy in its tomb, complete with all its treasures.

Howard started his mummy hunt in 1891, when he was seventeen. He took a job that would send him to Egypt to help the Egypt Exploration Fund copy ancient art before it decayed and was lost forever.

First, though, Howard spent a few months studying and sketching Egyptian art at the very proper British Museum in London. Howard, who was not very proper, was always in "a mortal funk lest my boots squeaked" and disrupted the quiet museum.

He was also in a funk on his
trip to Egypt, complaining about the
"smelly dining-saloon" aboard ship, his
"depressed state of mind" because he felt so alone,
and the awful seasickness that "centered around the
sensitive nerves of the solar plexus." But as soon as
Howard arrived in Egypt, his nose, mind, and solar
plexus felt better. He got to work.

MEDITERRANEAN SEA

BAHARI or LOWER EGYPT

Desert

OR CENTRAL EGYPT

ARABIA

GULF OF SUEZ

VOSTANI

Beni Hasan
Deir el-Bersha
Amarna
Hatnub

Valley of the Kings

SAID or UPPER EGYPT

EGYPT
1894.

BAHARI or LOWER E

NUBIA

Over the next few years, Howard traced and copied art for the Egypt Exploration Fund at many excavation sites, including the thirty-nine tombs at Beni Hasan, the rock-cut tombs at Deir el-Bersha, the ruins at Amarna, and the ancient quarries of Hatnub.

Howard was awestruck at the "dignity . . . restraint . . .
[and] beauty" of the art and architecture found at these sites,
but he was also impatient. How would he ever find a royal
mummy if he was only copying the things he saw? Somehow,
Howard had to learn the secrets of excavation.

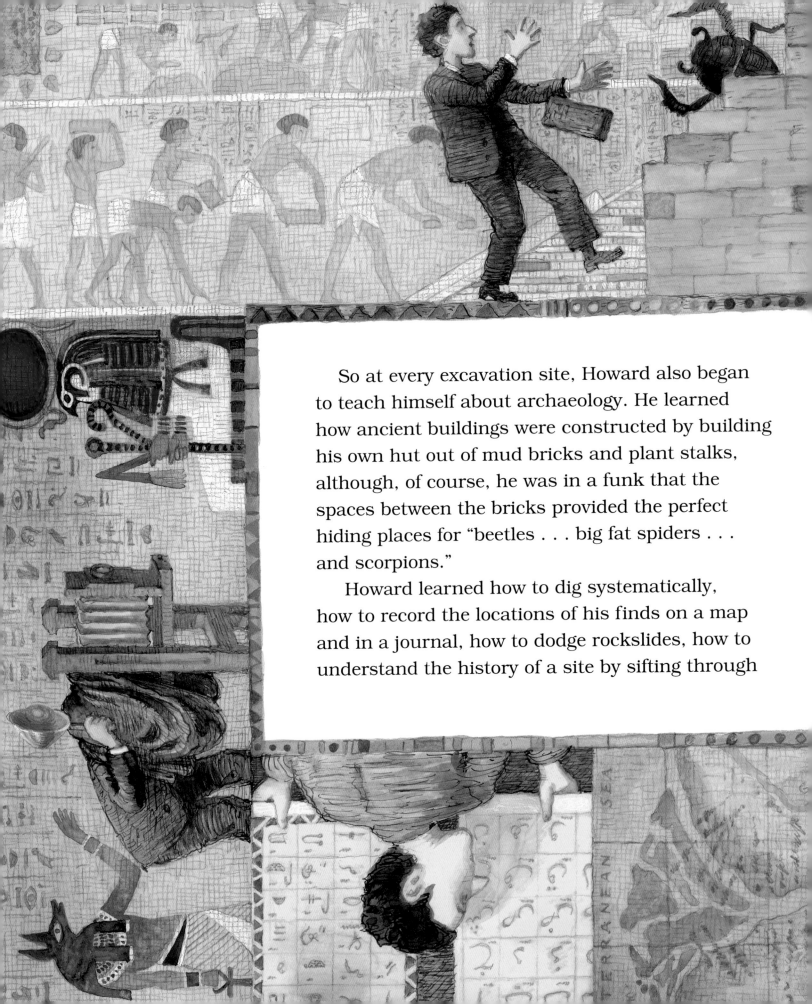

So at every excavation site, Howard also began
to teach himself about archaeology. He learned
how ancient buildings were constructed by building
his own hut out of mud bricks and plant stalks,
although, of course, he was in a funk that the
spaces between the bricks provided the perfect
hiding places for "beetles . . . big fat spiders . . .
and scorpions."

Howard learned how to dig systematically,
how to record the locations of his finds on a map
and in a journal, how to dodge rockslides, how to
understand the history of a site by sifting through

the layers of trash heaps, and how to preserve ancient cloth. He slowly taught himself how to speak Arabic so that he could communicate with his workers, and how to read hieroglyphics, the formal writing system used by ancient Egyptians.

Howard also studied photography, Egyptian history, geology, the patterns of flash floods, and the local wildlife. Howard said he felt like an insect going through its life cycle, slowly changing himself from a young artist into his "great desire . . . an excavator."

Howard's funky personality stayed the same. He admitted that he had a "hot temper" and a "terrible habit of neatness." Howard became famous for bellowing "Tommyrot!" at anyone who disagreed with him. One of his bosses grumbled that Howard was "obstinate." Even worse, a co-worker complained that Howard was so improper that he picked "his last . . . tooth with a match stalk during dinner."

In spite of his stubborn attitude and worse table manners, by now Howard was not only tracing and copying artifacts, he was also finding them: pottery shards, a gold ring, an unusual tablet, and two splendid statues of the pharaoh Akhenaten and his wife, Nefertiti. After years of hard work, Howard had turned himself into one of the best excavators in Egypt.

For several years beginning in 1899, Howard worked for the Egyptian government as Chief Inspector of Antiquities for Upper Egypt. He lived in what he jokingly called "Castle Carter," a small house on the west bank of the Nile. He had a favorite horse, Sultan, a gaggle of pigeons that he called his "messy mates," a few pet gazelles, and a beloved donkey, San-Toy, who often followed Howard inside Castle Carter, braying in delight.

Howard traveled up and down Egypt, arranging repairs to monuments, reporting on new discoveries, and supervising excavations. He was especially excited to oversee work for a man named Theodore Davis in the Valley of the Kings, an area near the modern city of Luxor, where many important royal tombs had been discovered. Howard even excavated several tombs only to find that they had been looted of most of their artifacts centuries earlier. Howard worried that he would never discover his royal tomb.

Then, in 1908, Howard met Lord Porchester, the fifth Earl of Carnarvon, better known as "Porchy." Porchy was a wealthy Englishman who also longed to find Egyptian treasures.

So far, Porchy had found only the mummy of a cat. Luckily, he could get along with anyone—even Howard. So, Porchy hired Howard to help him.

At the time, only Theodore Davis was allowed to organize digs in the Valley of the Kings. Davis was a wealthy American who was constantly crowing about his amazing discoveries.

Just a year earlier, Davis's men had uncovered a small pit that contained a few artifacts marked with a cartouche, an oval symbol that indicates that the heiroglyphics inside the oval are a royal name. The cartouche was translated as "Neb-Kheper-U-Re," one of the names of a little-known boy king who had ruled Egypt more than three thousand years earlier. Davis had also found artifacts marked with a different cartouche that was translated as another name for this same boy king: "Tut-Ankh-Amun, Ruler of Heliopolis and Upper Egypt." Davis boasted that he had found King Tutankhamun's tomb. He even published a book about it. Howard thought Davis's claim was absolute tommyrot!

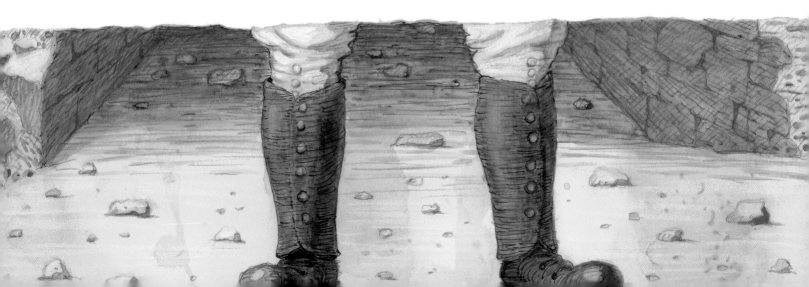

Howard believed the artifacts and pit were too small and unimportant to be a king's tomb. But if Davis hadn't found the real tomb of King Tut, where was it? Perhaps this would finally be the royal tomb that Howard had dreamed of finding! He started hunting.

Howard searched for the tomb for years. Since he couldn't dig in the Valley, he—and sometimes Porchy, too—excavated nearby. Howard even built a new house at Elwat el-Diban to be close by, and named it Castle Carter II.

The two men unearthed lots of artifacts: pottery, tablets, jewelry, a temple, several looted burial sites, and even some mummies. But they didn't find the missing tomb.

Then, in 1914, Davis announced that there was nothing left to discover in the Valley of the Kings. He retired. Finally, Howard and Porchy got permission to dig there. The search was on.

But Howard was once again in a funk. He found that searching the Valley of the Kings was "rather a desperate undertaking," since there were "mountains of rubbish" from previous excavations. Even worse, no one had ever kept accurate records of which areas had already been searched. Howard devised a plan.

First he drew a detailed map of the Valley of the Kings, dividing it into squares like a giant checkerboard. Then he marked the exact location of every previous find on his map. Howard decided to excavate every unsearched inch of the valley, square by square, right down to the bedrock.

He would work in the cool winter months before the desert became too hot even for camels.

In February 1915, Howard hired a crew of Egyptian laborers and got to work. Each morning, Howard dressed in a three-piece suit and his best homburg hat. He rode his donkey from Castle Carter II, down the rocky trail into the Valley.

There, he dug and sifted and dug and sifted. Usually he found only dust. But whenever he made even a small find, he carefully recorded it on his map and in his journal. Howard dug for a month until the desert became too hot.

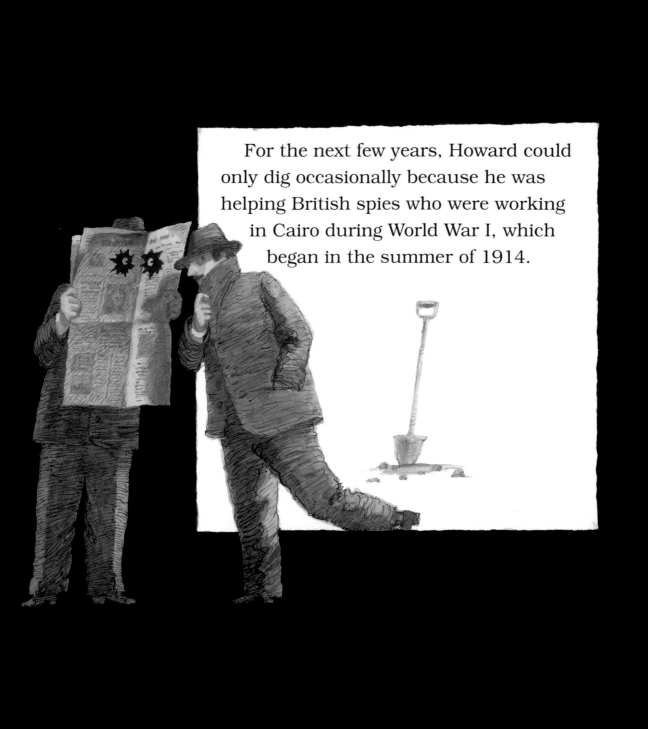

For the next few years, Howard could only dig occasionally because he was helping British spies who were working in Cairo during World War I, which began in the summer of 1914.

Despite his mysterious "war work," Howard managed to dig
in the Valley again in December 1917. This time, Howard dug
in a square that included the tomb of the pharaoh Ramses VI,
which had been excavated years earlier and was one of the
most popular tourist attractions in Egypt. This square was
piled so high with enormous heaps of sand, rock chips, and
boulders from previous excavations that Howard suspected no
one had ever thoroughly searched it.

Howard and his men had uncovered most of the square
when they ran into a small area that contained some ancient
workmen's huts. Excavating this area would have caused piles
of rubble to block tourists' access to the tomb of Ramses VI, so
they had to stop working. Howard had found only a few shards
of pottery.

About a year after the war ended in November 1918,
Howard started digging in a different spot. Porchy and his wife
arrived in February 1920 and dug, too. They found thirteen
alabaster jars, but they didn't find a tomb.

The next season, Porchy and his wife had returned to
England, so Howard dug without them from December 1920 to
March 1921. "Results nil," Howard wrote to Porchy.

In February and March of 1922, Howard dug every day.
He carefully noted many small finds, but he didn't discover a
tomb.

By now, Porchy, who was still back in England, was
ready to give up. Digging further was just too expensive and
uncertain. Howard thought that was tommyrot!

"So long as a single area of untouched ground remained the
risk was worth taking," Howard argued.

Porchy agreed to pay for one last season of digging. Howard studied his dusty map. At first glance, it seemed that he had already searched the entire Valley of the Kings. But there, near the tomb of Ramses VI, was the small area covered with ancient workmen's huts that Howard had not been able to search years earlier. He would never be satisfied until he had cleared that area, too.

So Howard started digging again on November 1, 1922. This was before the tourist season started, so his excavation would not interrupt sightseers' access to Ramses VI's tomb. Howard and his workers cleared away the ancient huts and began to remove the soil.

Three days later, a water boy sat down to rest. He
swept his hand through the sand—and felt a flat, smooth
piece of stone under the surface.

Could it be a step? Howard wondered.

Howard and his crew worked all that day and the next, uncovering another step—and then another and another . . . They found twelve steps in all, leading down into the ground.

Then Howard uncovered the top portion of a doorway. There! Howard spotted a faint seal pressed into hardened mud. The seal showed a jackal above nine bound men.

It was a royal seal! Howard carefully sketched it in his journal.
But was this a royal tomb, or just a royal storage room? Then
Howard noticed that a corner of the door had been broken and
later repaired and marked with a seal by keepers of the tomb
in ancient times. The seal was used by the tomb keepers to
indicate that robbers had gotten into the tomb long ago, and that
something valuable was still inside. But what?

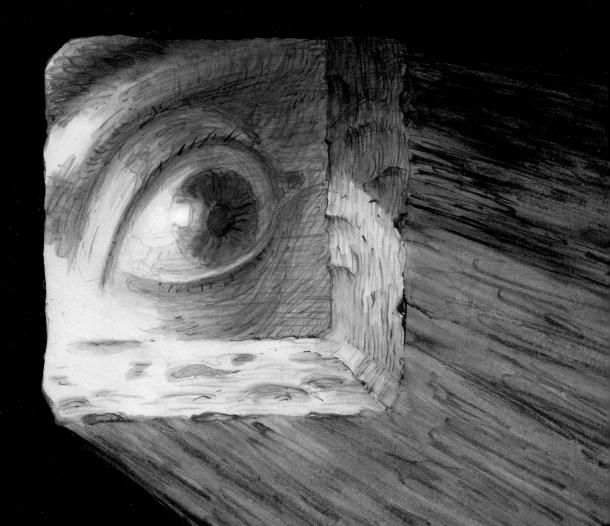

Howard cut a small hole in the upper
corner of the door and peered in. The passageway
was filled to the ceiling with rubble. Howard's heart
started to pound. This was how royal tombs had once
been protected from ancient robbers. The rubble was
another sign that whatever was inside was important and
had probably not been disturbed in a very long time.

By now, night had fallen. Howard posted guards at the spot. As soon as he could, he sent a telegram to Porchy in England:

"At last have made wonderful discovery in Valley . . . Congratulations!"

Then Howard mustered his patience to wait for Porchy and his daughter, Lady Evelyn, to arrive in Egypt.

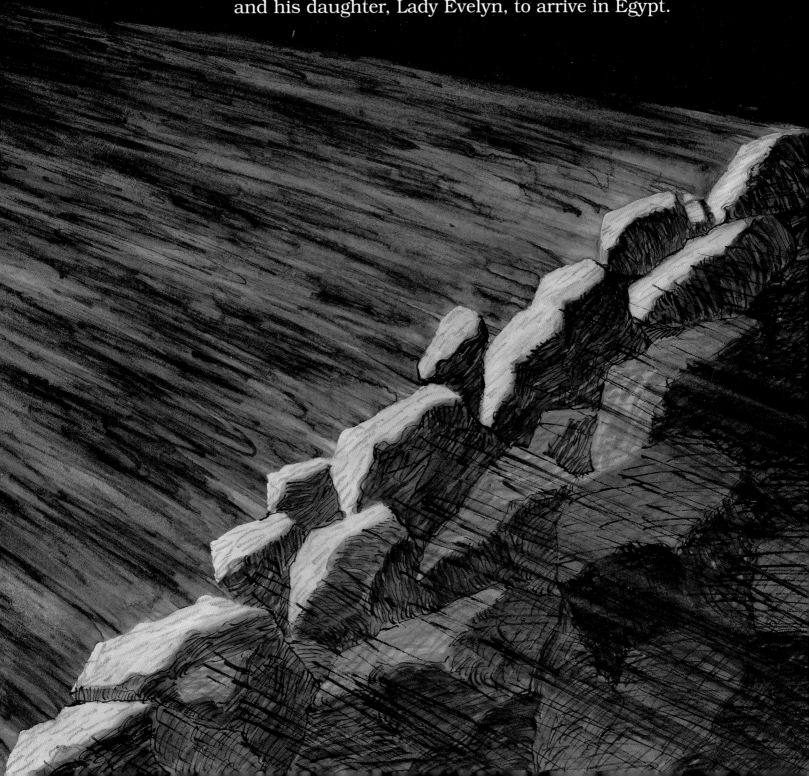

Finally, on November 24, 1922, Porchy and Howard uncovered four more stairs and the entire door. There, in the lower right-hand corner, Howard spotted a seal. In the center was a cartouche he recognized: Neb-Kheper-U-Re! Tutankhamun!

Howard carefully noted, sketched, and photographed the door.

He was so excited that he slept
at the tomb that night.

The next day, Howard opened the door.

He, Porchy, and their crew worked "feverishly"
to clear the rubble out of the dark, thirty-foot-long
passageway that led from the door down into the
ground. Then they came to another door. This door
had been broken and resealed in ancient times, too.

On November 26, Howard cut a small opening in this second door. His hand trembled as he thrust in an iron testing rod. There was nothing as far as his rod could reach. Howard knew, though, that poisonous gases sometimes collected inside underground tombs. He carefully widened the hole and stuck in a candle. *Whoosh!* The candle flickered but did not snuff out. That meant there was no poison gas.

By now, Howard's hands were shaking so hard he could barely work. He widened the hole, shone his electric torch inside, and slowly let his eyes adjust to the dim light.

"Can you see anything?" Porchy finally asked.

"Yes," Howard whispered. "Wonderful things!"

The chamber was stuffed with a "museumful" of treasures: two huge ebony statues of a king, a shrine filled with a terrifying snake, gilded couches decorated like fierce animals, finely carved chairs, a golden throne, and a heap of oddly shaped white boxes—a jumble of magnificent objects!

It was "the day of days, the most wonderful that I have ever lived through," Howard later said.

It took Howard nearly ten years to excavate the four-chambered tomb. It was the most complete and well-preserved tomb that had ever been discovered. Howard uncovered thousands of objects—everything from a flyswatter to a golden chariot—and sent them to the Museum of Egyptian Antiquities in Cairo. Best of all, inside four golden shrines, inside an enormous stone sarcophagus, inside three nesting coffins, beneath a magnificent twenty-two-pound solid gold mask . . . lay the 3,300-year-old mummy of King Tutankhamun.

Howard had finally found the royal mummy he had dreamed about since he was a boy.

AUTHOR'S NOTE

HOWARD CARTER was born on May 9, 1874, and grew up in the small town of Swaffham, England. He complained that he had a "miserably incomplete" education, but he was a talented artist who learned to sketch and paint from his father. Howard first discovered his love for Egyptian art at nearby Didlington Hall, the Amherst family manor, which had one of the largest private collections of Egyptian antiquities in England. The Amherst family most likely helped Howard get his first job in Egypt when he was only seventeen years old. Once there, he never wanted to leave.

At first Howard worked for the famous Egyptologist P. E. Newberry, copying art at Beni Hasan and Deir el-Bersha. Then he joined the equally famous archaeologist Sir William Matthew Flinders Petrie and began to learn the secrets of scientific excavation. Eventually, Howard became a very well-respected, although not always very well-liked, archaeologist himself.

Howard's discovery of King Tut's tomb was one of the most important archaeological finds ever made. He spent ten years carefully sketching, writing about, stabilizing, and removing more than five thousand objects from the tomb. Howard assigned every object—each splinter of wood and fragment of pottery—a number. Each numbered object was marked on a master plan and was also assigned a card that contained a full description, precise measurements, and detailed sketches. A colleague, Harry Burton, took hundreds of photographs that recorded every detail of the tomb and its artifacts. Many of Howard's fellow archaeologists thought Howard's attention to detail was "quite impossible!" but they also realized that his excavation was the most thorough and scientific that had ever been made.

After he finally finished excavating the tomb, Howard returned to England and became a collector for several museums. He died in 1939. Howard never wrote a complete autobiography, just some short personal sketches that often contained exaggerations or mistakes. Porchy, who had been in poor health for many years, died in 1923, just a few months after the discovery of the tomb. Some people wondered if his death was caused by a "mummy's curse" that doomed anyone who disturbed the tomb. Howard thought the myth of such a curse was pure tommyrot.

Today, much of Howard's painstaking work on the tomb, including his index cards, sketches, and maps, as well as the photographs taken by Harry Burton, can be viewed and searched online at the website of the Griffith Institute at griffith.ox.ac.uk.

SELECTED SOURCES

Allen, Susan J. *Tutankhamun's Tomb: The Thrill of Discovery.* New York: The Metropolitan Museum of Art, 2006.

Carter, Howard, and A. C. Mace. *The Discovery of the Tomb of Tutankhamun.* New York: Dover Publications, 1977.

James, T. G. H. *Howard Carter: The Path to Tutankhamun.* London: Tauris Parke Paperbacks, 2008.

Meyerson, Daniel. *In the Valley of the Kings: Howard Carter and the Mystery of King Tutankhamun's Tomb.* New York: Ballantine Books, 2009.

Reeves, Nicholas, and John H. Taylor. *Howard Carter: Before Tutankhamun.* New York: Harry N. Abrams, 1993.

Tutankhamun: Anatomy of an Excavation. The Griffith Institute website. griffith.ox.ac.uk/tutankhamundiscovery.html.

Tyldesley, Joyce. *Tutankhamen: The Search for an Egyptian King.* New York: Basic Books, 2012.